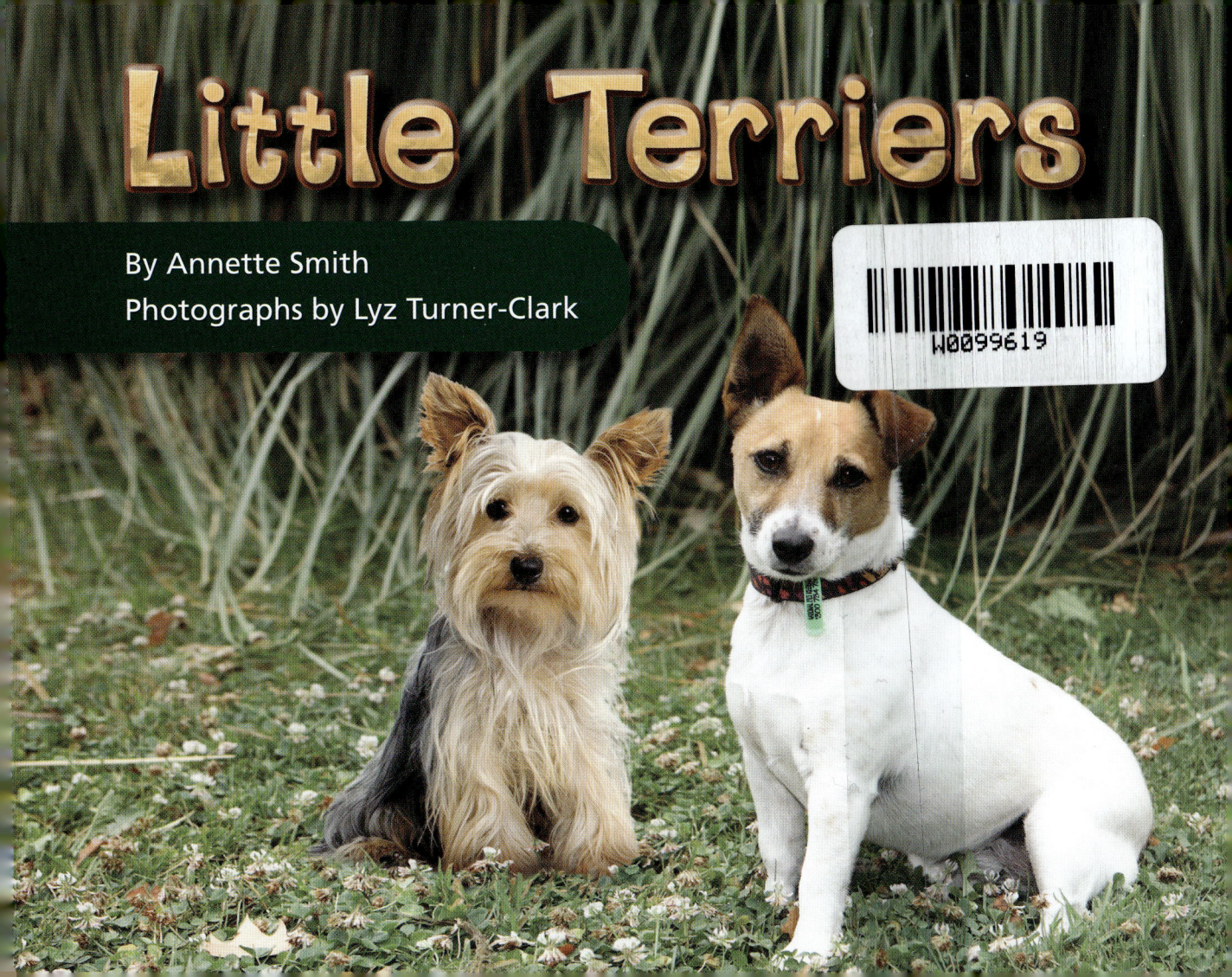

Little Terriers

By Annette Smith

Photographs by Lyz Turner-Clark

A terrier is a dog.

Some terriers are big.

Some terriers are little.

This is a little terrier.

It has little ears.

It has a little tail.

It has little legs, too.

little ears

little tail

little legs

Some terriers like to play.

This little terrier likes to play on the grass.

It runs after a ball.

This little terrier can run into a tunnel.

It sits in the tunnel.

Some little terriers are brave.

This little terrier is brave.

Some little terriers are naughty.

This little terrier is naughty.

Some little terriers are clever.

This little terrier is clever.

It is fun to play

with this little terrier.